A
Pocket
Guide
to
MAUI

text by **Curt Sanburn**
photography by **Douglas Peebles**

MUTUAL PU

Library of Congress Catalog Card
Number: 00-100525

First Printing, August 2000
Second Printing, March 2004
Third Printing, October 2005
3 4 5 6 7 8 9

Design by Jane Hopkins
ISBN 1-56647-159-1

Mutual Publishing, LLC
1215 Center Street
Honolulu, Hawaii 96816
Telephone (808) 732-1709
Fax (808) 734-4094
e-mail: mutual@mutualpublishing.com
www.mutualpublishing.com

Printed in Thailand

TABLE OF CONTENTS

KANOUNOU POINT

HONOLUA BAY   PO'ELUA BAY

HONOKOHAU

NAPILI BAY   KAPALUA   KAHAKULOA BAY
       NAPILI

HONOKOWAI

Whaler's   WAIHE'E
Village   Ka'ahumanu Church
        KA'ANAPALI   HO'OKIPA BEACH PARK   UAOA BAY
                              WAILUKU   Alexander &   PA'UWELA
Pioneer Inn   Baldwin   PA'IA BAY
Baldwin   Museum   HAIKU
House   KAHULUI   PA'IA
        LAHAINA   'IAO NEEDLE   ULUMALU
Carthaginian II   'Iao Valley
Ship Museum   State Park   Ke'a
Hale Pa'ahao   PU'UNENE   MAKAWAO   Arboret
Prison
                                                          PUKALANI
        OLOWALU

                M A'ALAEA   HALEAKAL
PAPALAUA   NATIONAL

        MA'ALAEA BAY
        Ka'ono'ulu Beach Park
                              KIHEI   KULA
        Kalama Beach Park   Kula Botanical
                                                          Gardens
        Kama'ole Beach Park
        Keawakapu Beach Park   HALEAKAL
                                          Polipoli Springs   NATIONAL
        Wailea Beach Park   WAILEA   State Recreation Area
                                    Tedeschi
                          MAKENA   Winery
                                                                    MAMALU
        Makena-La Perouse Bay   BAY
        State Park
                                                          KANALOA
        LA PEROUSE BAY   POINT
                KANAIO BEACH   KANALOA
                                    POINT

MAUI

FACTS & FIGURES

County: Maui, which includes the islands of Maui, Moloka'i, Lana'i, and Kaho'olawe

County seat: Wailuku

Land area: 728 square miles (Maui only)

Resident population: 115,163 (1995; includes Maui, Moloka'i and Lana'i)

Highest point: Red Hill, Haleakala, 10,023 feet

Shoreline: 120 miles

Extreme length and width: 48 miles by 26 miles

Average annual temperature: 74.35°F (Hana)

Highest recorded temperature: 98°F (Kihei)

Lowest recorded temperature (at sea level): 48°F; at Haleakala's summit: 14°F

Average annual rainfall at Kihei: 13 inches

Average annual rainfall at Pu'u Kukui, West Maui Mountains (about 10 miles from Kihei): 300 plus inches

Chief industries: visitors, construction, agriculture

Energy sources: 95% from imported oil

Hotel and condominium rental units: 17,711 (Maui only, 1998)

Visitors per year: 2,360,350 (Maui, Moloka'i and Lana'i)

Average number of visitors per day: 43,270 (Maui, Moloka'i and Lana'i)

Public and private golf courses: 9 (1998)

Public tennis courts: 39 (1998)

National Parks: 1

State Parks: 9 (Maui only)

County Parks: 115 (Maui only, 1998)

Recognized surfing sites: 212

'LA

NAHIKU

Pi'ilanihale Heiau

Wai'anapanapa State par

HANA

Hasegawa General Store

NAMOA

MU'OLEA

KIPAHULU   Seven Pools

ALTHOUGH "HOʻOKIPA" IS THE HAWAIIAN WORD FOR
HOSPITALITY, THE BEACH OF THIS NAME IS KNOWN FOR ITS
TREACHEROUS ROCK SHELF AND STRONG OCEAN CURRENTS—
MAKING IT DANGEROUS FOR SWIMMING, BUT PERFECT FOR
WINDSURING. MAJOR INTERNATIONAL WINDSURFING CONTESTS
ARE HELD HERE FROM OCTOBER TO APRIL. WINDSURFERS
CATAPULT INTO THE AIR, DO MIRACULOUS FLIPS AND SPINS, LAND
"SPLAT" ON THE WATER'S SURFACE, AND THEN JIBE THROUGH THE
WAVES AGAIN.

INTRODUCTION

THE CRESCENT-SHAPED ISLET OF MOLOKINI RISES 150 FEET OUT OF THE WATERS OFF KIHEI AND MAʻALAEA. ITS SEA-BREACHED CRATER WALLS HARBOR A SMALL BEACH JUST INSIDE THE PROTECTIVE "U" OF THE COLLAPSED VOLCANO. LEGEND HAS IT THAT THE ISLAND WAS ONCE A BEAUTIFUL WOMAN WHO WAS TURNED INTO STONE BY PELE, THE FIRE GODDESS.

✳   ✳   ✳   ✳   ✳

THE ISLAND OF MAUI gets its name from a mischievous, muscular Polynesian demigod, Maui, who stole the secret of fire from the gods and slowed the sun's flight across the sky so Hawaiian days would be longer and warmer.

Like its namesake, the island of Maui revels in the sun and devotes its long days to playful and athletic pleasures. It is the most glamorous and flamboyant of all the Hawaiian Islands. With miles of swimming beaches, two perpetually sunny coasts, awesome mountains, and calm, leeward seaways ringed by a scenic fleet of lesser islands, Maui has every right to its gilded reputation, its international allure, and the phrase used to describe it: *"Maui no ka ʻoi,"* Maui is the best!

Maui, the second youngest and the second largest of Hawaiʻi's eight major islands, includes in its 728-square-mile landmass two distinct volcanic domes—mighty Haleakalā ("House of the Sun") and the compact West Maui Mountains. Haleakalā rises 10,023 feet above sea level, while the older West Maui Mountains have a maximum height of 5,778 feet at the top of Puʻu Kukui. The two eroded volcanoes are joined by central Maui's broad, flat isthmus, formed about a million years ago when lava from Haleakalā met the shores of West Maui. The isthmus functions as a broad valley between the peaks; thus, Maui's nickname, "the Valley Isle."

Offshore are four junior islands, all part of Maui County. Sleepy Molokaʻi struggles to maintain its rural character. Lanaʻi was recently transformed from a

AT MAUNAWAINUI, ALONG THE
WINDWARD CLIFFS OF HALEAKALĀ
BETWEEN KIPAHULU AND KAUPO,
DOZENS OF RAIN-FED WATERFALLS
CARVE A SERIES OF DEEP RAVINES AND
HANGING VALLEYS. SPLASH POOLS
COLLECT THE CASCADING WATER
AND FUNNEL RUNOFF TOWARD THE
OCEAN THOUSANDS OF FEET BELOW.

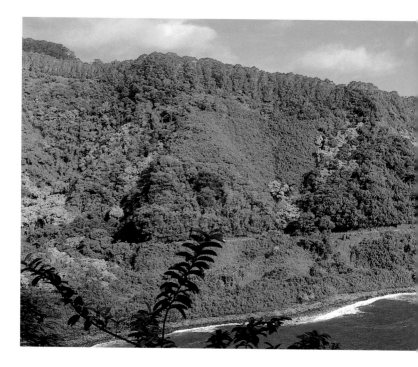

pineapple plantation to an exclusive private resort. Kahoʻolawe was a U.S. Navy bombing target for many years. And Molokini, a tiny crescent-shaped volcanic cone, is very popular as a snorkeling destination.

Together with the Big Island of Hawaiʻi, Maui was the stage for ancient Hawaiʻi's most important events and wars. An era of peace between the rival chiefs of Maui and Hawaiʻi gave way in the 1600s to two centuries of endless bloodshed. The Maui dynasty of Kekaulike and his son Kahekili was finally defeated in 1790 by the powerful chief from the Big Island, Kamehameha the Conqueror.

By 1802, Kamehameha had unified all the Hawaiian Islands except Kauaʻi (which he obtained peacefully in 1810). As the first king of a united Hawaiʻi, he established his royal capital at Lahaina on Maui's leeward coast.

To show his respect for the superior Maui bloodlines, and to secure those bloodlines for his royal heirs,

SLICED INTO THE LUSH GREEN COAST OF EAST MAUI, THE WINDING ROAD TO THE REMOTE PARADISE OF HANA TOWN IS FAMOUS FOR ITS DANGEROUSLY NARROW HAIRPIN TURNS, WATERFALL-MISTED GULLY BRIDGES, STANDS OF GIANT BAMBOO, FERN GROTTOES, AND SPARSELY POPULATED VALLEYS.

Kamehameha married two of Maui's most chiefly women: Ka'ahumanu and the sacred princess Ke'opuolani. After his death, his Maui queens retired the old Hawaiian gods and, at the urging of their Protestant missionary advisors, led the Hawaiian conversion to Christianity. *Heiau,* the simple stone temples of Hawaiian worship, were torn down and replaced by churches and schools, where texts printed in the Hawaiian language taught spiritual and practical learning.

Whales put Maui on the map 150 years ago, when whalers from the eastern U.S. and Europe used the safe and convenient anchorage at Lahaina for a central provisioning stop in the whale-rich northern Pacific. As many as 400 ships dropped anchor there every year during the 1840s. Grog shops and lawlessness proliferated, along with commerce and growth. At the time, Lahaina's native and foreign population was about 3,500 people and 528 dogs.

The discovery of petroleum in Pennsylvania in 1871 put an abrupt end to the whale oil business and the whaling fleets. The royal seat of the kingdom was moved to the larger commercial port at Honolulu on O'ahu. Lahaina was all but deserted.

For the next century, Maui slumbered as its vast lands were consolidated into sugar cane and pineapple plantations, and its mountain streams were tapped for irrigation water. Until the early 1960s, Maui was little more than a few plantation camps, cattle ranches, isolated fishing villages, a half-dozen spartan hotels, and plenty of space. The sugar fields spread uninterrupted like rich lawns from the foot of the mountains to the beaches.

The tourist boom began at Ka'anapali in 1962. For the next 25 years and continuing today, resort hotels, golf courses, and vacation condominiums have seemed to sprout up wherever there is a sunny swimming beach. Little Kahului airport, long accustomed to a few inter-island flights daily, found itself welcoming nonstop jumbo jets direct from mainland U.S. cities.

✻   ✻   ✻   ✻

ONCE A BUSTLING PORT OF CALL FOR THE WHALING INDUSTRY OF THE MID-PACIFIC, LAHAINA HARBOR IS NOW HOME TO A SMALL FLEET OF CHARTER FISHING BOATS AND PLEASURE CRAFT. THE RED-ROOFED PIONEER INN IS A GENTLE REMINDER OF THOSE BAWDY DAYS OF RUM AND SCRIMSHAW.

At the same time, mainland hippies found the deeper meaning of "mellow" on Maui's remote beaches and in the smoky haze of its famous *pakalolo* (marijuana). The island became a world-renowned playground for the Age of Aquarius.

The current Maui atmosphere attracts large numbers of "life-stylists" to the island's seaside condominiums and chic Upcountry cabins. These folk settle down for a few years as realtors, hotel bartenders, carpenters, small shop owners, and trust-fund windsurfers. As a result, Maui is the fastest growing and most heavily *haole* (Caucasian) of all the islands.

About two-and-a-half million visitors now spend $1.5 billion on Maui each year. On an average day, 42,000 visitors share the island with a resident population that has passed the 100,000 mark. Locals grumble about traffic that most newcomers barely notice.

Amid all the glitzy resorts and swank restaurants, Maui manages to keep its island character and its soaring beauty alive. To be enjoyed are its natural and man-made wonders, its country roads, ancient temples, peaceful beaches, blazing sunsets, misty rains, friendly smiles, and dewy flowers.

HAWAIIAN PINCUSHION PROTEA CATCH THE SUN.

OPPOSITE: THIS INTREPID PARA-SAILING HUMAN KITE DANGLES FROM A COLORFUL PARACHUTE ABOVE THE INTER-ISLAND CRUISE SHIP, THE *OCEAN INDEPENDENCE.*

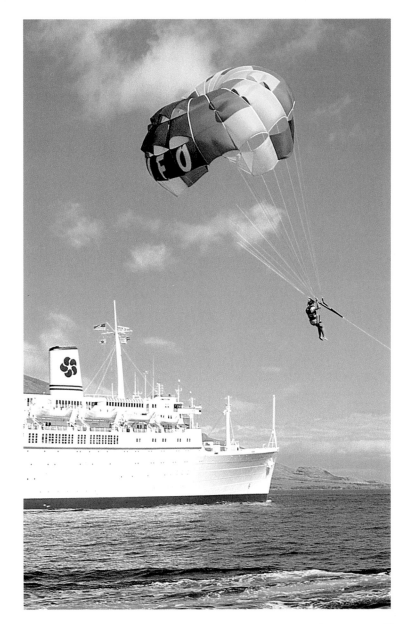

La Perouse Bay on the southernmost tip of Maui, just below the ʻUlupalakua Ranch, lies well past civilization. Stunning cobalt blue water contrasts with the stark black of Haleakalā's most recent lava flow (dated around 1790). The French explorer La Perouse reported a shallow bay in this area in 1786. It was mapped and named by Captain George Vancouver a few years later. From this aerial angle, the West Maui Mountains loom as an apparition in the distant background.

VIGNETTES

Early Reports from the Explorers

"About a hundred and twenty persons, men and women, waited for us on the shore.... The women showed by the most expressive gestures that there was no mark of kindness they were not disposed to confer upon us, and the men in the most respectful attitude endeavored to discover the motive of our visit in order to anticipate our desires.... I had no idea of a people so mild and attentive."

—from the journal of French navigator Jean Francois Galaup, Comte de la Perouse, who on May 30, 1786 made the first European landing on Maui at Keone'oi'o, now known as La Perouse Bay.

"...They have coarse features, thick eyebrows, black eyes which without being hard express self-confidence, prominent cheekbones, slightly widened nostrils, thick lips, a large mouth, and teeth which are somewhat wide but quite fine and straight. Their hair is black and cut in the pattern of a helmet. Worn very long, like the flowing crest of a helmet, their hair is a reddish brown color at the ends.... These people paint and tattoo their skin. They pierce their ears and nasal septa, and adorn themselves with rings inserted in these parts.

"The inhabitants in general however are mild and engaging in their behavior, and even show toward strangers a degree of politeness.... The dress of both sexes consists of a sort of apron covering what nature bids them conceal, and another piece of similar cloth wrapped around the body."

—from the journal of Dr. Rollin, physician aboard La Perouse's flagship Boussole.

The Sugar Plantations

Brought as a food plant by the Polynesians, sugar cane, a giant grass, was first grown in the Islands commercially in 1802. The enterprise failed. Forty years later, when the California Gold Rush and the American Civil War spurred demand for sugar, large plantations were established here, often on former chiefly and royal lands. A reciprocity treaty with the U.S. reduced import duties on Hawaiian sugar, and by 1890 Hawai'i was exporting 250 million pounds of sugar a year.

Labor was a problem; Hawaiians, ravaged by disease and culture shock, were unable to adapt to plantation life. The plantation owners looked to China, then to the Portuguese islands of Madeira and the Azores, and to Japan, Korea, and the Philippines for workers. Between 1852 and 1948, roughly 300,000 contract laborers arrived to work the twenty-seven plantations spread across Hawai'i's arable land. When their contracts were up, most of them stayed. The plantations have dwindled, but the descendants of the workers have flourished.

Today the old plantation camps are historically akin to New York's Ellis Island—the place where poor and often frightened people had their first taste of life in a strange and wonderful new land.

THE GENTLY ROLLING FENCE-LINED RURAL ROADS OF UPCOUNTRY MAUI HAVE THE APPEARANCE OF MIDDLE-AMERICA, EXCEPT FOR THE DRAMATIC OCEAN VIEWS OFFERED AT EVERY TURN.

✻   ✻   ✻

The Spectacular Protea— Upcountry's Most Exotic Export

Upcountry Maui's rich, well-drained volcanic soil, its warm days and cool nights, and its mix of rain and sun create perfect growing conditions for an amazing family of ancient flowering plants called protea (pro-tee-uh). With multi-layer, multi-texture, and multi-color blossoms, proteas surely rank among the plant world's most elaborate demonstrations of nature's art.

The extraordinarily diverse protea family (more than 1,500 species and varieties have been catalogued) derives its name from the Greek sea god Proteus, who was able to transform himself into any form he desired. Proteas grow wild in their native South Africa and Australia. The outrageous blossoms created a sensation when European adventurers brought them to the attention of French and British botanists in the eighteenth century. Both England's King George III and Napoleon's Empress Josephine took up hothouse protea cultivation as a hobby.

The flowers were brought to Maui in the early 1960s by pioneering University of Hawai'i botanist David Williams. He planted fifty species on the Kula slopes of Haleakalā. An almost immediate commercial success, the durable, colorful blossoms command high prices both locally and in mainland U.S. markets, bringing international recognition to Hawai'i's flower industry.

Roughly fifty species of protea and related banksia grow in Upcountry flower farms. Their colorful names suggest the blossoms' spectacular possibilities: the giant king protea, the giant woolly-beard, woolly-headed protea, the rose-spoon protea, the pink mink, the ermine tail, the candlelite, the Hawaiian sunburst pincushion, the red swamp banksia, the pink star, the silver tree, the flametip, the safari sunset, the woolly banksia, the golden acorn, the raspberry frost, the orange frost.

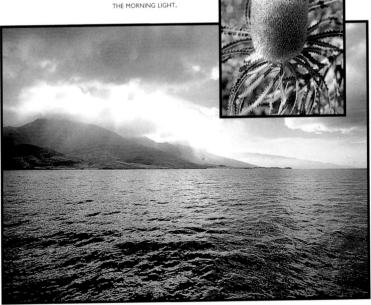

A GOLDEN BANKSIA GLOWS IN THE MORNING LIGHT.

BACKLIT BY SUNRISE, A CLOUD BANK PLUMES OVER THE WEST MAUI MOUNTAINS. THE SOUTHEASTERN SPUR OF HALEAKALĀ IN THE DISTANCE IS THE SITE OF THE LAST LAVA FLOWS ON THE ISLAND.

THE DESOLATE INTERIOR OF HALEAKALĀ HAS BEEN
COMPARED TO THE SURFACE OF THE MOON. THIS VIEW
FROM NEAR THE VISITORS' CENTER FACES NORTHEAST
TOWARD THE KOʻOLAU GAP AND ITS NEAR-CONSTANT
CLOUD POCKET. ON THE LEFT RISE THE JAGGED SPIRES
OF THE LELEIWI CLIFFS, AND ON THE RIGHT THE
KALAPAWILI RIDGE AND ITS HIGHEST POINT,
HANAKAUHI PEAK.

NATURAL SPECTACLES

MYTHOLOGY NOTWITHSTANDING, THE 1,600-mile-long chain of the Hawaiian Islands was built by volcanic action beginning roughly 30 million years ago at Kure Atoll, at the northwestern end of the archipelago, and continuing today on and near the Big Island at the southeastern end of the chain. A slow, steady northwestern drift of the earth's upper layer over a deeper "hot spot" accounts for the island chain's linear shape and the progressive age of the islands within the chain.

The typical landform is the broadly rounded "shield" volcano, built up from the ocean floor to heights in excess of two miles above sea level by innumerable thin lava flows. Mauna Loa on the Big Island is a classic—and still active—shield volcano, so gentle in its rise that its 13,600-foot height (as high as most Rocky Mountain peaks) is difficult to appreciate.

On the eight major islands, it's easy to see the geological evolution from the broad, swelling shapes of young and virtually intact shield volcanoes on the Big Island to the heavily eroded, jagged topography of Kaua'i. Low-lying Ni'ihau island is the almost completely worn-down remains of an even older shield volcano.

On Maui, the dominating mass of dormant Haleakalā clearly shows the broad shape of a "young" shield volcano (active as recently as 200 years ago). By contrast, the originally compact West Maui volcano is so deeply dissected that it is now referred to as the West Maui "Mountains." The separate "peaks" are actually the surviving shoulders of the volcano, cut by deeply-eroded canyons. Viewed from Makena, however, the West Maui landmass can be seen to retain its overall shield-volcano shape.

The effects of rainfall and resulting stream erosion are most striking on the windward (northeastern) sides of all the islands. Windward Haleakalā and West Maui, particularly at 'Iao Valley, show heavy stream erosion. Leeward slopes, where much less rain falls, show relatively little.

Trade wind-driven waves have carved low sea cliffs all along Maui's exposed northeastern coastline. On nearby Moloka'i, the same waves have carved cliffs higher than 2,000 feet, among the highest in the world, on the north shore of the island.

THE KE'ANAE PENINSULA ON THE HANA COAST IS FAMOUS
FOR ITS PRODUCTION OF *TARO*. HERE A SMALL *LO'I* OR *TARO*
TERRACE IS NESTLED NEAR THE RUGGED COAST ON THIS
HEAVILY VEGETATED SPIT OF LAND.

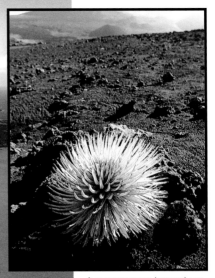

A SILVERSWORD *KEIKI* (SEEDLING), LIKE A SPIKY BALL OF DULL PLATINUM, GLISTENS AGAINST THE RUGGED VOLCANIC TERRAIN OF HALEAKALĀ.

PU'U 'OLA'I ("RED HILL") CINDER CONE, ON A JUTTING PIECE OF LAND SEPARATING THE SOUTH MAUI COAST FROM THE BACK SIDE OF HALEAKALĀ, IS FLANKED BY MAKENA'S LITTLE BEACH AND BIG BEACH (ONELOA). THIS UNDERDEVELOPED AREA, ONCE ZONED FOR RESORTS, WAS ACQUIRED FOR A STATE PARK IN THE LATE 1980S AFTER A 15-YEAR COURT BATTLE.

GOING SOUTH PAST HANA, NEAR THE END OF THE PAVED ROAD, ARE THE SEVEN POOLS. THIS NATURAL SUCCESSION OF SMALL WATERFALLS TUMBLING INTO BASE POOLS CONTINUES IN A CONSTANT FLOW TO THE OCEAN. THE POPULAR SWIMMING HOLES ARE A REFRESHING STOP AFTER THE LONG AND SOMETIMES TORTUROUS DRIVE DOWN THE HANA ROAD. THE ANCIENT PEOPLE NAMED THESE POOLS 'OHE'O, AND PLACED A KAPU ON THEM THAT PROHIBITED MENSTRUATING WOMEN FROM BATHING IN THE TRANQUIL WATERS.

RAPID CHANGES IN ALTITUDE AFFECT YOUR BREATHING, AS YOU
WIND YOUR WAY INTO THE MIDDLE OF A VAST, DESOLATE, CONE-
BLISTERED CUP LINED WITH VOLCANIC RUST-COLORED CINDER
DEVOID OF VEGETATION OR LIFE.

TOURS
HALEAKALĀ'S UPCOUNTRY

Either a morning drive up the dormant volcano, with lunch in Kula on the way down, or a full day's outing to take in all of the mountain's top-to-bottom wonders is a must. While the all-day drive is a strenuous one, it offers everything of interest—including a long, but unforgettable, drive to the spectacular "Dismal Coast" on Haleakalā's south flank. Get an early start.

LEFT: CRATER ROAD ZIGZAGS THROUGH MAUI'S "CLOUD COUNTRY" TOWARD THE 10,023-FOOT SUMMIT OF HALEAKALĀ (HOUSE OF THE SUN).

BELOW: GENERATIONS OF UPCOUNTRY *PANIOLO* PROUDLY CARRY ON TRADITIONS INTRODUCED TO HAWAI'I BY MEXICAN VAQUEROS. THESE "ESPAÑOL" WERE BROUGHT TO THE ISLANDS IN 1803 TO HELP ROUND UP FERAL HORSES AND CATTLE GIVEN TO KAMEHAMEHA THE GREAT.

The drive up through the clouds and the view from the top of Haleakalā are among the best reasons to visit Maui. Starting in Kahului, Route 37, the Kula Highway (377) and Haleakalā Highway (378) climb past sugarcane fields, emerald truck farms, ranchlands, mist-wrapped stands of eucalyptus and fir, high grasslands, and, above the 7,000-foot cloud line, the alpine shrublands and lava deserts of the summit. Overall, the thirty-eight mile, ninety-minute drive climbs two vertical miles, one of the shortest and fastest high-mountain climbs on earth.

At 6,800 feet is the entrance to Haleakalā National Park, which requires a modest entrance fee. Proceed to the Visitor Center perched above Haleakalā, where a truly awesome landscape of cinder slopes and multi-colored volcanic cones floats above a sea of clouds. Off to the southeast, the volcanic peaks of the Big Island rise. Far below and to the west are the islands of Kahoʻolawe, Lanaʻi, and Molokaʻi; on very clear days, even Oʻahu can be seen. Self-guided walks along the crater rim, hikes

IT IS SAID THAT WHEN THE FIRST SPANISH-SPEAKING VISITORS SAW THIS PIECE OF LAND ON THE SIDE OF HALEAKALĀ, THEY EXCLAIMED, "O LINDA VISTA" (OH, BEAUTIFUL VIEW). OLINDA, A CLASSIC STORYBOOK HAMLET OF PASTURES AND FARMS, IS NESTLED JUST SOUTH OF THE SCENIC MEADOWS OF HALEAKALĀ DAIRY AND HALEAKALĀ RANCH. STANDS OF EUCALYPTUS TREES ARE LACED THROUGH THE GREEN PASTURES OF THIS UPCOUNTRY COMMUNITY.

✻   ✻   ✻

into the crater, as well as guided overnight hikes and horseback trips, are possible. It is important, however, to have proper shoes or boots and rain gear, as the weather can change abruptly for the worst, particularly in the crater. (For weather information, contact the park headquarters at the visitor center.)

Watching the sun rise from the summit of Haleakalā is an almost mystical experience. However, get on the road not later than 4 a.m. (5 a.m. during winter months) for the two-hour drive, to arrive at the top in time for the pre-sunrise aurora and subsequent light show. DRESS WARMLY. Wear long pants and take a sweater or jacket—even a hotel blanket.

After the spectacle of sunrise has passed and the light is strong, visit the park head-quarters just inside the park entrance to learn the lore of Haleakalā and to catch a glimpse of Hawaiʻi's state bird, the endangered *nene* goose. The unique and wonderful silversword plant is most easily seen in the vicinity of the Kalahaku

ABOVE: BUILT IN 1897 BY PORTUGUESE LABORERS, THE OCTAGONAL BUILDING OF THE HOLY GHOST HALL OF OUR LADY QUEEN OF ANGELS CHURCH STANDS ALONE PAST THE SMALL TOWN OF KULA, NEAR WAIKALOA.

LEFT: HORSES, INTRODUCED TO THE ISLANDS BY TRADERS SEEKING ROYAL FAVOR, MULTIPLIED IN THE WILD UPLANDS OF THE BIG ISLAND AND MAUI.

overlook turnoff, two miles below the Haleakalā Visitor Center.

Kula Highway and Route 377 follow the 2,000-foot elevation around Haleakalā's western slope through the Kula and 'Ulupalakua countryside. These roads are Upcountry's garden boulevards, where scores of small carnation, chrysanthemum, protea, Kula onion, and lettuce farms create a deeply-colored patchwork. Pastures, stands of eucalyptus, and open grasslands spread out beyond the irrigated plots to frame a panorama of the ocean and the rest of Maui lying far below. As if all this were not enough, from April to June the green fields and roadsides are brushed with the luminous lavender flowers of jacaranda trees.

Upcountry has become an important nursery center for exotic plants and flowers. The Sunrise Protea Farm at the bottom of the Haleakalā Highway (378) near its inter-section with Route 377 is a good spot to see cultivated protea. The cut flowers can be mailed anywhere in the United States as gifts.

Two other spots for viewing Maui's exotic flora are the Kula Botanical Gardens on Route 377, two miles

THE ERDMAN-TEDESCHI VINEYARDS, NESTLED AMONG MAJESTIC STANDS OF EUCALYPTUS, PRODUCES THE ONLY COMMERCIAL WINE IN THE ISLANDS.

✳   ✳   ✳

south of Route 378, and the University of Hawai'i's Kula Experimental Station on Copp Road, off the Kula Highway.

Beyond the 'Ulupalakua cattle ranch around the southwestern shoulder of Haleakalā, Kula Highway becomes Pi'ilani Highway (31). Near 'Ulupala-kua Ranch head-quarters, among green pastures and groves of eucalyptus, are the beautiful grounds of Tedeschi Vineyards. Wine tastings, offering a Hawaiian *Blanc de Noir*, a "Maui Blush," or a novelty pineapple wine, are held in a restored old jailhouse near the highway. The winery is open from 9 a.m. to 5 p.m.

Narrow, bumpy Pi'ilani Highway skitters around Haleakalā's southwest volcanic rift zone, well above the beach resorts at Wailea and Makena, into a prehistoric landscape—what French explorer La Perouse called the "Dismal Coast" when he first saw it in 1786. Haleakalā's vast dry southern flank sweeps relentlessly from the two-mile-high summit to an empty, gale-lashed coast. One or two ranches, barely noticeable in the vastness, share the sparse grazing. Cattle wander carelessly over the road.

Across the stormy 'Alenuihaha Channel, the rounded volcanoes of the Big Island, eighty miles south, hang in the sky.

Despite its story-book nickname, the Dismal Coast was home to thousands of Hawaiians when the first westerners arrived. Fishing settlements dotted the rocky coast, and villages growing sweet potatoes and *taro* spread their lava-rock foundations across upland meadows. Freshwater springs determined the location of these settlements.

Extensive stone terraces, the remains of the village of Kahikinui ("Great Tahiti"), command a plateau a thousand feet above the sea. From Manawainui Gulch, where the Pi'ilani Highway finally descends to sea level, an ancient shoreline trail marked by lines of stones crosses the barrenness all the way to La Perouse Bay. Three miles beyond Manawainui, at Nu'u Bay, thickets hide the symmetrical rock piles and petroglyphs of a long-abandoned fishing village and its canoe launching site.

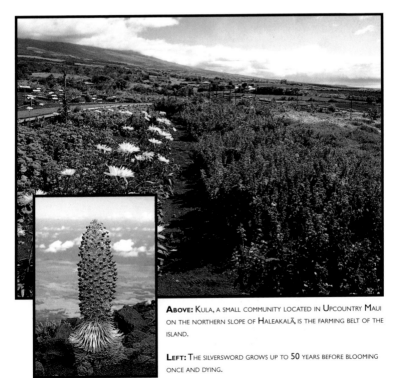

ABOVE: KULA, A SMALL COMMUNITY LOCATED IN UPCOUNTRY MAUI ON THE NORTHERN SLOPE OF HALEAKALĀ, IS THE FARMING BELT OF THE ISLAND.

LEFT: THE SILVERSWORD GROWS UP TO 50 YEARS BEFORE BLOOMING ONCE AND DYING.

Hundreds of former house sites (little more than rock piles now) line the coast. Because there has been very little disruption here, the haunting sense of being close to the past is strong along the Dismal Coast. Is that just a rockpile, or a sign of former human life? Who arranged these stones? What joys and sadnesses were lived out on these awesome shores? What gods were conjured up to match the harsh grandeur of this land and sea?

From Nu'u Beach, the road climbs a promontory capped by the stone platform of an ancient *heiau*. Less than a mile beyond Nu'u, a broad, flat lava peninsula, Lapehu Point, juts into the surf below. On the windswept point can be seen several symmetrical stone formations, the remains of a fishing shrine. If you still have the energy, and enough daylight remains, the half-hour hike down to the point is a fitting end to your Haleakalā tour . In visiting the site, remember to be respectful in all ways.

Two miles beyond Nu'u Bay the road becomes impassable, and you must turn around for the long drive back to the twenty-first century.

ON A TINY SURF-POUNDED PENINSULA BELOW THE KAUPO RANCH IS THE LONELY WHITE CORAL BUILDING OF HUIALOHA (A "GATHERING OF LOVE") CHURCH. COMMONLY KNOWN AS THE KAUPO CHURCH, THIS OLD CONGREGATIONAL MEETING HOUSE WAS ORIGINALLY BUILT IN 1859, A TIME WHEN KAUPO WAS ALMOST TOTALLY LANDLOCKED, ACCESSIBLE ONLY BY SEA AND A PRIMITIVE TRAIL. AN UNLOCKED GATE AT THE ROAD LEADING TO THE CHURCH WELCOMES ALL TO VISIT THE GROUNDS.

SELLING EVERYTHING FROM PRE-
PACKAGED *TI* LEAF CUTTINGS TO MANGO
CHUTNEY, TINY SPECIALTY SHOPS, LIKE THE
SUNRISE PROTEA STORE IN UPCOUNTRY,
CATER TO THE RENT-A-CAR TOURISTS
WHO BRAVE THE WINDING ROADS OF
HALEAKALĀ'S SLOPES.

LA PEROUSE BAY, NAMED BY CAPTAIN
GEORGE VANCOUVER IN HONOR OF
FRENCH EXPLORER LA PEROUSE. A
DRAMATIC VIEW OF NATURE'S
CONTRASTS—THE GLISTENING, SHALLOW
BAY EMBRACED BY HARDENED LAVA WHICH
LAST FLOWED FROM HALEAKALĀ AROUND
1790—IS CAPTURED IN THIS BIRD'S-EYE
VIEW.

THE CINDER CONE CLUSTER OF PU'U O MAUI ("HILL OF MAUI"), HALALI'I (NAMED FOR AN O'AHU TRICKSTER
DEMIGOD), AND PU'U NAUE ("EARTHQUAKE HILL") ALL STAND WITHIN THE CENTER OF HALEAKALĀ.

HORSES GRAZE IN THE HIGH PASTURES OF
'ULUPALAKUA RANCH.

THE HANA COAST IS RENOWNED FOR ITS EXCELLENT FISHING
GROUNDS. THE LAND, POURED OUT IN LAYERS FROM NUMEROUS
ERUPTIONS OF HALEAKALA, PLUNGES STEEPLY TO GREAT DEPTHS,
CREATING THE DRAMATIC CONTRAST OF VERDANT CLIFFS, JET BLACK
LAVA AND LAPIS-BLUE WATER. THE HAZARDS OF FISHING AND DIVING
IN THESE AREAS DUE TO SUDDEN HIGH SURF AND SHIFTING CURRENTS
HAVE TAKEN MANY LIVES, BUT HAVE NOT SLOWED THE HARVEST OF
THE OCEAN'S BOUNTY.

HANA & THE SOUTHEAST COAST

THE DANCERS OF HAKU MELE O HANA PERFORM THE *KAHIKO* (ANCIENT) HULA AT THE HANA MAUI HOTEL.

*　　　*　　　*　　　*　　　*

SET ASIDE A FULL day for exploring the Hana Coast. Take a swimsuit and towel, mud shoes, and an umbrella or rain coat—just in case—as this is the wettest coast of Maui. For more information on the Hana coast, see *Maui's Hana Highway* by Angela Kay Kepler (Mutual Publishing.)

The two-hour drive (minimum) to Hana from Kahului follows a notoriously winding, narrow road. Traffic bound for Hana peaks at midmorning; the return rush is between 4 and 6 p.m. The trip, as spectacular as it is, can be exhausting.

An alternative schedule to beat the traffic is to begin your trip at midday, eat dinner in Hana, and return in the evening. Driving the Hana Highway at night is not that bad. For most of its length, the road is well marked with reflectors and stripes; headlights of oncoming cars can be seen for hundreds of yards in the darkness. Another possibility, and by far the most relaxed way, is to make advance reservations and spend the night in Hana at the Heavenly Hana Inn, Hana Bay Vacation Rentals, Hana Kai Condominiums, or at any of Hana's handful of small motels or vacation rentals. Driving can then be spread over two days, allowing quality time for exploring the scenic and historic corners of Maui's Garden of Eden.

The tour starts at lower Pa'ia Town on the Hana Highway. Pa'ia, an old plantation "camp," was once a major population center until the master-planned suburbs of Kahului attracted most of its workers away after World War II. The town reawakened in the late 1960s to a gentle invasion of hippies, artists, and other free spirits who spruced up its fading storefronts and added an artsy-craftsy, tofu-and-sprouts overlay. Today colorful Pa'ia is an international meeting place for wind-surfers who tackle the big waves and steady winds nearby.

A good place for breakfast, Pa'ia is also the last chance until Hana to fill your gas tank. Then buckle your seat belt and get set for the narrow, 52-mile Hana Highway. Untainted land-scapes around every curve, waterfalls by the score, (more than 600 of them), fifty-six bridges, and over-whelmingly rich tropical vegetation are the special pleasures. Watch the mile markers to locate several of the sights described here.

Another thing: Commuting over the tortuous Hana Highway is a daily ordeal for local residents. Please *kokua* (co-operate) and pull over quickly when someone wants to pass.

Baldwin Beach Park, just west of Pa'ia, and Ho'okipa Beach Park, just east of the town, are two popular beaches on the Hana Highway with wonderful views across the water to the West Maui Mountains. Baldwin is a local favorite, while Ho'okipa is a world famous windsurfing spot known for high-performance wave riding, especially in the winter months. Spectators have a good view from the parking area above the bay, but the water is not recommended for inexperienced swimmers, except in the shallow pools right at beachside.

Beyond the settlements of Ha'iku and Huelo, the road climbs and twists above the sea cliffs, gulches, and bays

CRASHING SURF AND BARE LAVA OUTLINE THE KE'ANAE PENINSULA. IT IS SAID THAT THE GOD KANE THRUST HIS SPEAR INTO A ROCK AND A FRESH-WATER SPRING GUSHED FROM THE HOLE. ONCE THE SITE OF MANY FISHPONDS, THE PENINSULA REMAINS A COMMUNITY OF *TARO* FARMERS.

✳   ✳   ✳

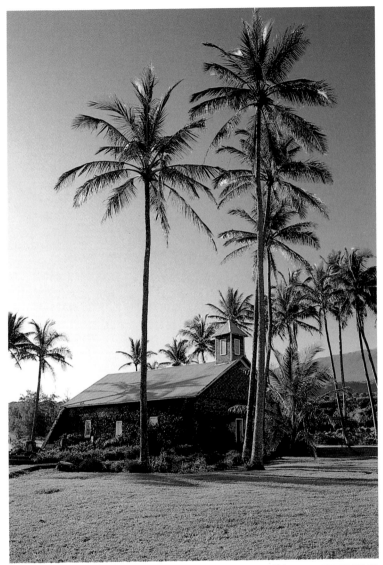

WITHIN EARSHOT OF THE GRINDING SURF ALONG THE RAGGED EDGE OF LEAF-SHAPED KE'ANAE PENINSULA SITS ONE OF THE EARLIEST OF THE CIRCUIT CONGREGATIONAL CHURCHES BUILT ON MAUI. ERECTED IN 1856, THIS CHAPEL SURVIVED THE 1946 TIDAL WAVE THAT CLAIMED THE LIVES OF SEVERAL OF ITS CHURCH MEMBERS.

to Kailua's neatly-tended gardens, and the small dams and ditches of the East Maui Irrigation (EMI) system. By that time, the sugar cane, pineapple, and pasturelands of agricultural Maui have given way to the mostly introduced species of Maui's windward lowland forests. Ironwoods, Norfolk Island pines, *kukui*, guava, mountain apple, African tulip, and *hau* shelter an understory of ferns, gingers, heliconias, and allamanda. Fabulously fragrant white, yellow, and *kahili* ginger blossoms are worth picking if you see their delicate, stringy flower clusters set amid thick green banks of paddle-shaped leaves on long stalks. A handful of ginger on your car dashboard will pump out its sweet scent all day.

For eat-ing, lemon-size yellow-to-pink guava fruit is conspicuously abundant on roadside bushes. Though seedy, the sweet, mild fruit can be eaten like an apple, skin and all. Small, red-to-pink mountain apples, which ripen in late summer and early fall, are juicy with a pear-like taste. Unfortunately, they tend to hang just out of reach.

UMBRELLA-SHADED TABLES AND LOUNGE CHAIRS GRACE HAMOA BEACH, ONCE A RECREATION AREA MAINTAINED FOR THE EXCLUSIVE USE OF WEALTHY HOTEL HANA MAUI GUESTS. NESTLED INTO THE VERDANT HANA COAST, THIS PEARLY WHITE BEACH IS NOW OPEN TO THE PUBLIC.

✻   ✻   ✻

A forest canopy of bunchy, soft-green treetops rippling in the wind introduces the Waikamoi region's bamboo forests. At ground level, bamboo stands are dark, impenetrable, and tightly spaced, often broken by the ghostly diagonal lines of fallen stalks. The wind rustles the leafy tops, but inside the grove all is silent. It's no wonder Buddha is said to have loved bamboo forests.

An excellent place to get personal with a tropical forest is the Waikamoi Ridge Trail, one-half mile beyond mile marker 9. The turnout and trail are well marked. On the trail, look for solid, deep red, tightly petalled blossoms about the size of a child's fist. These are *'awapuhi,* or "shampoo ginger." Squeeze the smooth, shiny blossom and a thick, sticky liquid, used by Hawaiians as a shampoo/hair conditioner, appears. A national line of expensive hair-care products now uses *'awapuhi* in its formulations, so you may as well give it a try. Apply the unscented gook to wet hair, comb through, then rinse. One blossom is enough for a head of hair.

LOOKING LIKE COLORFUL SINGLE-WINGED BUTTERFLIES FLUTTERING THROUGH A GARDEN OF BLUE AND WHITE FLOWERS, WINDSURFERS PLY THE WAVES AT WORLD-FAMOUS HO'OKIPA. THE 1946 TIDAL WAVE REDUCED THIS ONCE CAPACIOUS STRETCH OF WHITE SAND TO A NARROW BEACH FACED WITH A ROCKY SHELF.

THE HIGH SURF AND SWIRLING CURRENTS OF HO'OKIPA BEACH PARK ARE A FAVORITE PLAYGROUND FOR THE WORLD'S TOP WINDSURFERS. THESE ADVENTUROUS WAVE RIDERS CUP THE 30-KNOT TRADE WINDS IN THEIR MYLAR SAILS AND HEAD STRAIGHT FOR THE FACE OF A 10 TO 15-FOOT CRESTING WAVE.

WAI'ANAPANAPA, ONE OF MAUI'S FEW BLACK-SAND BEACHES, IS THE MOST POPULAR FEATURE OF THE WAI'ANAPANAPA STATE PARK JUST OUTSIDE OF HANA. A *HULA HALAU* (DANCE TROUPE) GATHERS AT LOW TIDE FOR A CEREMONIAL INVOCATION TO THE ANCIENT GODS.

The scenery, particularly the waterfalls, begins to intensify beyond Waikamoi. At Puohokamoa Stream, a pullout (probably with a few cars parked) marks a double waterfall, as well as a swimming pond, reachable by a short trail. (Note: Do not drink free-flowing water anywhere on this coast. Wild upland pigs have brought dangerous bacteria into the watershed.)

You are halfway to Hana when you reach Kaumahina State Wayside Park, where there are beautiful views of Honomanu Bay and Ke'anae peninsula, a short nature trail, picnic tables, drinkable water, and restroom facilities.

Look for the *hala* trees here and all along the rest of your drive, recognizable by their tropical, prehistoric look. Smooth-skinned, patterned limbs rise from exposed bunches of stilt roots to support a canopy of thick, spiralling tufts of shiny, spine-edged leaves. These lovely, romantic trees once covered huge windward areas of all the islands and were essential to the Hawaiians as

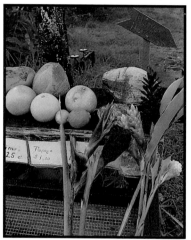

THIS ROADSIDE DISPLAY OF COUNTRY MERCHANDISING OFFERS A VIVID LOOK INTO MAUI'S RURAL CULTURE.

✳   ✳   ✳

sources of building materials, medicines, matting, and fishing supplies. Durable *lauhala* mats, made from the stripped, softened, and plaited leaves, were used everywhere until World War II. Unfortunately, the craft of *lauhala* weaving is disappearing.

As you approach the Ke'anae peninsula, at a sharp hairpin turn, the Ke'anae Arboretum is clearly marked on the *mauka* (mountain) side of the road. Maintained by the Hawai'i State Department of Land and Natural Resources, this free facility has a highly informative presentation of Hawai'i's native plants, introduced plants, traditional Hawaiian food-stuff, and material source plants.

Beyond the bucolic Ke'anae peninsula, home to a small, private community of Hawaiian *taro* growers (whose fields are best viewed from an overlook near mile marker 17), there is a rapid succession of waterfalls. Fruit stands sell bananas, papayas, coconuts, mountain apples (in season) and star fruit. Pua'a Ka'a State Park, just beyond tiny Wailua, is a good stopping point.

The highway then climbs to 1,200 feet, the highest elevation on the road.

The final "must" stop before Hana is the 120-acre Wai'anapanapa State Park, just beyond the Hana Airport. This popular park offers camping and cabins (permits and reservations needed), a dramatic black-sand beach set in a jagged lava cove, and a series of freshwater caves, reachable by a well-marked trail from the upper parking lot. When the water is calm, snorkeling is excellent. Remnants of the old *alaloa*, long trail, that once circled Maui is found near the caretaker's house, and can be followed on foot along the sea cliffs, or all the way into Hana town.

Ancient stone walls, marking Polynesian house sites, *heiau*, and gravesites abound here and should be treated with care. Throughout Hawai'i, it has become common to wrap a small stone in a *ti* leaf and leave it in the forest or directly on old stone walls to show respect for the spirit of a place. Offerings left by others should not be disturbed.

One of Hawai'i's loveliest and most remote outposts, the historic garden community of Hana is a relaxing luncheon stop after the dizzying drive. Visit the friendly (and tiny) Hana Cultural Center (Hale O Waiwai O Hana), the beachfront at Hana Bay for good swimming and views of legendary Ka'uiki Hill, and the spot in the middle of the bay where Hawaiians have surfed for centuries.

A VAULTED TUNNEL OF SHOWER TREES AND BOUGAINVILLEA.

To the right of the pier a short but difficult path leads out to Ka'uiki Head and the lighthouse beyond. The path passes the birth cave of Hawai'i's most historically influential female *ali'i*, Ka'ahumanu, the favorite wife of King Kamehameha. She encouraged the abandonment of the ancient *kapu* (taboo) system. Then drive up Lyon Hill to Fagan Memorial Cross (visible from the highway in the center of town) for the panoramic view of the entire coast. If the gate is closed, inquire at the Hotel Hana-Maui, whose lobby is across the road.

Hotel Hana-Maui serves a moderately expensive a la carte lunch, highly recommended, if only for a glimpse of life at one of the world's idyllic hideaway resorts. Other lunch options include the Hana Ranch Restaurant further up the road, or Tutu's snack shop down by the bay for burgers.

If you still have energy, head on to Hamoa Beach, 100-foot Wailua Falls, and the popular Seven Pools of 'Ohe'o Gulch in the Kipahulu section of Haleakalā National Park, twelve scenic miles beyond Hana. (At this point, who's counting?) A clearly marked parking area puts you close to the 'Ohe'o Stream and its many shallow swimming pools. Below the bridge near the ocean are the most popular pools. Adventurers head up along the slippery stream bed half a mile to Makahiku Falls, and Waimoku Falls a mile beyond that. The trek can be dangerous in rainy weather; read the signs carefully and check with the ranger on duty to be sure.

The often washed-out road beyond Kipahulu is off-limits to rental cars. Turn around here and head slowly back to a good night's rest.

THE WIND-TOSSED SUGAR CANE FIELDS OF PIONEER
PLANTATION STRETCH FROM THE RESORT AREAS OF
KAʻANAPALI AND LAHAINA TO THE FOOTHILLS AND
VALLEYS OF THE WEST MAUI MOUNTAINS.

WEST MAUI

MAUI'S MILES OF SUNNY south and west-facing shoreline were perfect for developing a new visitor industry. These shores are sheltered from the prevailing northeast trade winds; the sun is predictable, the waters calm, the rains infrequent, the sunsets sublime; and the outlying islands—Moloka'i, Lana'i, and Kaho'olawe—give scenic depth to the horizon.

In the late 1950s, the owners of the Pioneer sugar mill chose three miles of white-sand beach at Ka'anapali, just north of Lahaina, as the place to begin West Maui's transformation into a major international

BUILT IN 1901, LAHAINA'S HISTORIC PIONEER INN PRESIDES OVER THE WATERFRONT ACTIVITIES AT TOWN SQUARE ALONG WHARF STREET.

❈ ❈ ❈

resort destination. The opening of the Royal Lahaina Resort in 1962 and the Sheraton Maui Hotel a year later launched Maui's development as a visitor destination.

The West Maui tour begins beyond Ka'anapali at the far end of Honoapi'ilani Highway, where a handful of dramatic cove beaches scallop the shore. In succession southward, the coves include Honokohau Bay, Punalau, Honolua (Maui's premier winter surf spot), Slaughterhouse, and D. T. Fleming Beach Park. All but Fleming are unmarked, except for cars parked along the road. Access to the beaches is by steep paths. The water, usually rough in winter, is great in summer for snorkeling and swimming. Fleming Beach has parking, showers, and restrooms.

THIS POLYCHROMATIC SEA CAPTAIN BY ARTIST REEMS MITCHELL IS A RELIC OF AN ERA LONG GONE. STANDING ON THE PORCH OF LAHAINA'S PIONEER INN, THE OLD SALT SURVEYS THE HARBOR AND SILENTLY POSES FOR PICTURES WITH ANY TOURIST WHO COMES HIS WAY.

✻   ✻   ✻

Past Fleming, the highway widens through the manicured Kapalua resort area. The Kapalua Bay Hotel and Villas and the Ritz Carlton Kapalua are Maui's premier resorts, a ranking assured by its turquoise-to-royal-blue water, its white-sand beaches, and its tremendous views across blustery Pailolo Channel to East Moloka'i. The exclusive Ironwoods subdivision at Oneloa Beach is home to C.E.O.s, film and music stars, and other notables. Inland, tall stands of Cook Island pines give distinctive charm to two golf courses.

Follow the main road until it becomes Lower Honoapi'ilani Road where it enters the Napili resort and residential area. The half-mile strip of low-rise hotels and condos here is flanked by gardens and serene beaches.

The broad, excellent Napili Bay swimming beach is accessible by several hard-to-spot rights-of-way between the condos and hotels.

The land-mark Napili Kai Beach Club, a low-rise luxury hotel at Napili Bay's northern end, is one of Hawai'i's increasingly rare "old-fashioned" hotels. Its modest design, simple interiors, and beautifully planted grounds harmonize with, rather than try to overwhelm, the environment.

The three miles between Napili and Ka'anapali are full of high-rise condo apartments and private homes. Many of West Maui's most reasonably priced beachfront rentals are at Kahana and Honokowai.

Ka'anapali was once a heavily-cultivated taro producing region, then a shipping point, and, finally, a dump for the nearby Pioneer Mill. Today, it is a world-renowned resort. Six luxury hotels and several condominiums line the beach and highway, carefully spaced to allow for gardens, pools, tennis courts, and shopping arcades.

To reach the central resort area, turn off Honoapi'ilani Highway into the second entrance, clearly marked "Ka'anapali Beach Resort." Parking for non-guests is limited, but usually available, at the Hyatt and the Westin Maui, near the Sheraton, and at Whaler's Village. By law, landowners must provide public access to the beach, but nothing was said about parking!

There is excellent snorkeling off Pu'u Keka'a (Black Rock), site of the Sheraton Maui Hotel. The beach is the fantasyland of the Hyatt Regency Maui and Whaler's village, with great restaurants, forty-five shops, and a whaling museum nearby. All along the beach is golden sand, calm water (in summer), and views across 'Au'au Channel to the gently rounded island of Lana'i.

An important part of Ka'anapali's master-planned success is its proximity to Lahaina, a real town with a real seafaring history akin to New England seaports like Nantucket and Provincetown.

Continue south on Honoapi'ilani Highway to Lahaina ("merciless sun"). Follow Front Street past the Jodo Mission (its huge Buddha and ancient palms are worth a stop) and Lahaina's shops, restaurants, and galleries. Just beyond the busy waterfront lies the heart of the old town, located at the landmark Pioneer Inn (circa 1901), the huge banyan tree planted in 1873, and the harbor. A block further down Front Street, at the corner of Prison Street, is a public parking lot. Park the car for a one-to-two-hour walking tour.

Lahaina's history is fascinating. In prehistoric legend, an ancient king begat a daughter, Kihawahine, who on her death became a great *mo'o*, lizard-goddess. She apparently lived in a pit

On the shores of Ka'anapali, windsurfers enjoy the fading ember of the Maui sun.

on a small island called Moku'ula, in a pond near the present Prison Street parking lot. The pond and island were considered sacred and remained important royal sanctuaries until the mid-nineteenth century. The pond was filled in 1918 for athletic fields and a playground. (Note: Even today, respect for lizards is a basic Hawaiian emotion.

The accidental deaths in door jambs of little household *geckos* are considered tragic.)

When Kamehameha the Great united the islands, he paid respect to the sacred bloodlines of Maui's chiefs by marrying two Maui princesses and establishing his royal capital at Lahaina. The foundations of his "Brick Palace,"

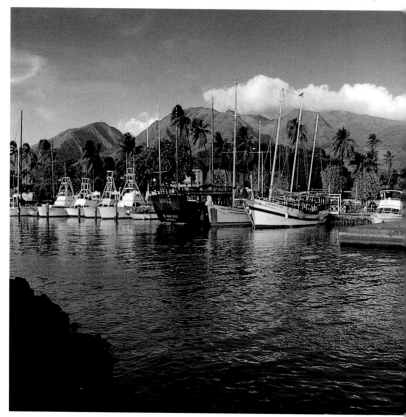

LAHAINA HAS PLAYED A MAJOR PART IN ISLAND HISTORY FOR MORE THAN 300 YEARS; FIRST, AS A FAVORED RECREATIONAL SPOT OF HAWAIIAN ROYALTY, THEN AS THE ARENA FOR THE CONFLICT BETWEEN THE RAUCOUS WHALERS AND PIOUS MISSIONARIES. LAHAINA TODAY IS ONE OF THE WORLD'S PRIZED PLAYGROUNDS.

built in 1802 as the first European-style building in Hawai'i, are visible near the sea wall in front of the public library, next to the Pioneer Inn. Too hot to live in, the palace functioned as a warehouse.

The effects of the arrival of New England missionaries in the 1820s, followed by the whaling fleets, remain the most visible and celebrated chapters in the town's colorful past. For a complete recounting, read *Lahaina: Royal Capital of Hawaii* by Roy Nickerson; for a self-guided walking tour of Lahaina's thirty-one designated historic sites, a free booklet is available at the Pioneer Inn or at the Lahaina Restoration Foundation offices.

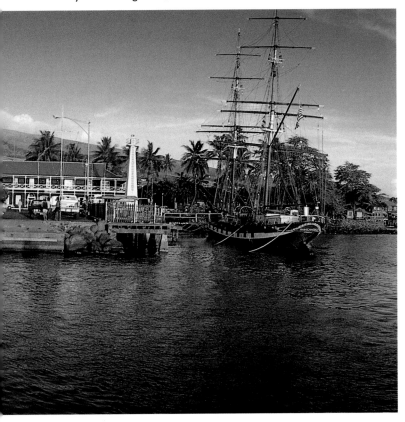

Returning to Honoapi'ilani Highway, head south toward Central Maui. For fifteen miles the highway skirts the narrow, reef-fringed beaches of Puamana, Launiupoko, Kulanaokalai, 'Awalua, Olowalu, Ukumehame, and Papalaua. The first four beaches are popular for swimming and sunning; Puamana, Launiupoko, and Papalaua have public facilities.

As the highway climbs over the 'A'alaloloa sea cliffs to the Papawai Point scenic lookout, Molokini, Kaho'olawe, and Lana'i islands stand in full view, as well as Haleakalā's southwestern coastline from Kihei and Wailea to the prominent volcanic cone, Pu'u Ola'i, at Makena.

From October to early April, the waters off Papawai Point are prime calving, nursing, and mating grounds for the humpback whales that commute each year from their Alaskan and Siberian summer feeding grounds. The whales visit all the Hawaiian Islands, but the spacious waters protected by the four islands of Maui, Moloka'i, Lana'i, and Kaho'olawe attract the largest concentration. Papawai Point lookout is the premier vantage point to watch these special visitors spouting and breaching in the sun.

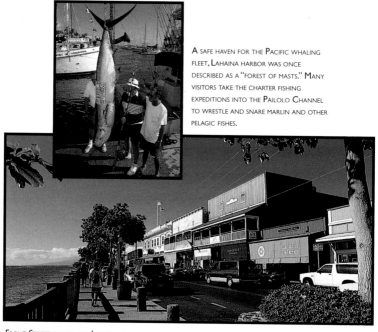

A SAFE HAVEN FOR THE PACIFIC WHALING FLEET, LAHAINA HARBOR WAS ONCE DESCRIBED AS A "FOREST OF MASTS." MANY VISITORS TAKE THE CHARTER FISHING EXPEDITIONS INTO THE PAILOLO CHANNEL TO WRESTLE AND SNARE MARLIN AND OTHER PELAGIC FISHES.

FRONT STREET IN HISTORIC LAHAINA TOWN STILL RETAINS MUCH OF THE CHARM OF THE OLD WHALING DAYS.

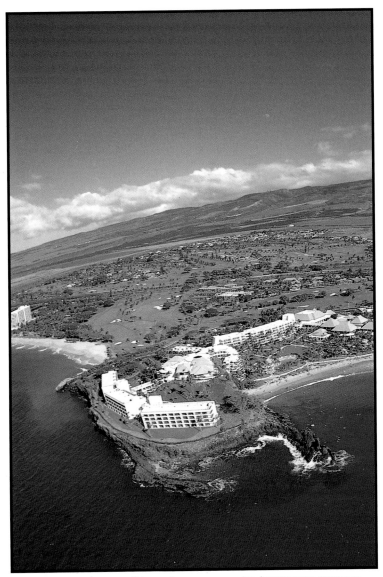

ALONG THE WHITE SANDY STRETCH OF KAʻANAPALI BEACH, EVERYDAY IS SUMMER. AT THE FAR RIGHT ARE THE TWIN TOWERS OF THE WHALER ON KAʻANAPALI BEACH RESORT.

THE NEW RESORT COMMUNITY OF WAILEA, ON THE SOUTHWESTERN SIDE OF HALEAKALĀ, BOASTS GRAND HOTELS, CONDOMINIUM CLUSTERS, AND A NUMBER OF CHAMPIONSHIP GOLF COURSES. DEVELOPED BY THE ALEXANDER & BALDWIN CORPORATION IN THE LATE 1970S AND 1980S FROM 10,000 ACRES OF FORMER MATSON NAVIGATION COMPANY RANCH LAND, THIS AREA IS ONE OF HAWAI'I'S MOST RECENT DESTINATION RESORT DEVELOPMENTS. THE CONGLOMERATION OF BUILDINGS IN THE DISTANCE AT LEFT IS THE TOWN OF KIHEI.

SOUTH MAUI

THE RICH FLAXEN-COLORED HUES AND SHIMMERING TANGERINE HORIZON OF A SOUTH MAUI SUNSET.

❊   ❊   ❊

START AT MA'ALAEA, SOUTH of Lahaina, where Route 31 branches from Hono-api'ilani Highway. Head southeast toward Kihei. The two-lane highway passes the long stretch of windy Ma'alaea Beach (great for expert wind-surfing and long walks). Inland from the highway is the Kealia Pond bird sanctuary.

Kihei is probably the most California-influenced community in Hawai'i. Its boomtown atmosphere and youthful population give the area a crackling energy. Kihei offers the most affordable living on Maui. Its relatively inexpensive subdivisions and condos are home to many Canadian "snowbirds," avid fans of Kihei's no-nonsense accommodations and perfect weather. These birds show up every winter.

Six beach parks along Kihei Road provide relief from the town's condo row. The best for swimming and quiet sunning are Kama'ole Beach Parks I, II, and III, at the south end. Most refreshing about Kihei is its sheer vitality. It's a normal town in a fabulous location. Nothing is master-planned, and almost nothing is controlled. It's exuberant and inclusive, rather than tasteful and exclusive.

South Maui is known for top-notch diving. If you are a scuba or snorkel prac-titioner, join a tour to Molokini Islet, a tiny, volcanic crescent about three miles off the coast. Or, if you are qualified, plunge in on your own, particularly off the rocky points of Wailea and Makena. (Your hotel activities desk will have more information.)

THE UNIQUE OBSTACLES OF JAGGED 'A'A LAVA, AS HERE AT HOLE #8 OF THE WAILEA RESORT'S ORANGE COURSE, MAKE SAND TRAPS SEEM ALMOST PLEASANT.

✳   ✳   ✳

Farther south on Kihei Road, the condos give way to private homes on new streets. Suddenly you're in Wailea, a master-planned 1,450-acre hotel resort. The heavily irrigated land-scaping is lush (in its natural state, this was a near desert), and the understated road signs remind you that this is no ordinary sub-division. Three golf courses, with homes facing the fairways, and several condominium complexes complete the tastefully framed picture. The luxury beachfront hotels include Stouffers, the Intercontinental, Grand Wailea, the Four Seasons Resort, Outrigger Wailea Beach, the Grand Wailea Kealani, and the Renaissance Wailea Beach Resort.

Wailea's five perfect cove beaches—Keawakapu, Mokapu, Ulua (the most popular), Wailea, and Polo—are among Maui's best for swimming and snorkeling. The access routes are clearly marked on Wailea Alanui Drive, the main road through the resort.

Beyond Wailea lie some of Maui's nicest, least crowded beaches offering beautiful sunset views. Offshore is stark, low-lying Kaho'olawe island, subject of a long-running dispute between Maui's Protect Kaho'olawe Ohana and the U.S Navy, which was finally ordered to cease its practice bombing of Ka-ho'olawe late in 1990.

South on Wailea Alanui Drive, past the hotels, is old Makena Road and several small, undeveloped but extremely worth-while beaches. Palauea Beach is the best—a flat, wide, and completely undeveloped crescent of sand just south of Polo Beach.

The road continues through the *kiawe* thicket to Po'olenalena Beach Park, a small, sandy cove with parking, and then to the charming beachfront Keawalai Congregational Church, built of coral lime stone in 1832. From the shady churchyard with its turn-of-the-century gravestones, the view of the little rock-framed cove is exquisite.

Returning from the churchyard, go *mauka* to Wailea Alanui Drive. Follow the drive south, past the entrance to the Maui

Prince Hotel, the most recent of Maui's lavish golf resorts. Just beyond the hotel the road turns bumpy and narrow. On your right, watch for Pu'u 'Ola'i volcanic cone, the area's principal landmark. Two dirt roads lead to the right, the second to Oneloa Beach, better known as Makena or Big Beach, Maui's outstanding undeveloped beach. A small cove on the ocean side of Pu'u 'Ola'i, Oneuli or Little Beach, is the island's most popular clothing-optional beach.

Beyond the left or south end of Big Beach, a low, black-lava point reaches into the sea. This is the tip of Maui's only recent lava flow, which apparently occurred in 1790. French explorer La Perouse reported a shallow bay here in 1786. Six years later British explorer Capt. George Vancouver mapped a large, protruding lava point in the same area, separating the present Makena Beach from La Perouse Bay.

At the south end of Makena the remains of an old fishing village are worth finding and exploring—if you have sturdy shoes. The village site, Maonakala, is within the 'Ahihi-Kina'u Natural Area Reserve. Follow the paved road beyond Makena to where the pavement dissolves into gravel. Keep going past the sign for the reserve, where the lava field begins. A dirt road on the right leads to a path to your left as you face the ocean. The village is among the *kiawe* trees a few hundred feet away. Remnants of the old King's Trail, which used to circle the island, are visible in the lava fields.

La Perouse Bay, at the end of the road, has a string of sandy pocket beaches which are also good for snorkeling in calm weather, but be careful of *wana*—sea urchins—in the shallow waters. The road is impassable beyond the bay.

THE SETTING SUN OVER MA'ALAEA BAY AND KAMA'OLE BEACH NEAR KIHEI.

A COOL, GENTLE BREEZE, THE SWISH AND RUSTLE OF PALMS, AND A HAMMOCK ON THE BEACH ARE THE MAKINGS OF A PERFECT SOUTH MAUI VACATION. CARES OF THE WORLD CAN'T PENETRATE THIS KIND OF BLISSFUL SOLITUDE.

THESE CHILDREN FLASH AN UNDERWATER "SHAKA" SIGN (HAWAIIAN HAND GREETING) WHILE SNORKELING IN MOLOKINI ISLET'S LAGOON.

SOUTH OF KIHEI AND AROUND THE PROTRUDING PROMONTORY OF PU'U 'OLAI, IS THE GENEROUS EXPANSE OF SAND KNOWN AS BIG BEACH. IN THE BACKGROUND, THE WEATHERED VOLCANIC TUFTS OF HALEAKALĀ'S SOUTHERN FLANK SLOPE TOWARD THE SEA.

CENTRAL MAUI

BUILT IN 1841 BY MISSIONARY EDWARD BAILEY AS A
FAMILY HOME, THIS SMALL MUSEUM IS NOW CALLED
HALE HO'IKE'IKE.

＊　　　　＊　　　　＊

ABOUT **30,000** PEOPLE, one-third of Maui's total population, live in Wailuku and Kahului, the twin towns between the West Maui Mountains and Maui's north coast. Older, picturesque Wailuku, the Maui County seat, is upland near the mouth of 'Iao Valley; Kahului is a growing port and commercial town with shopping centers, service businesses, and distributor warehouses. These stolid, seemingly un-remarkable middle-class communities deserve a closer look. This is where real people live.

Wailuku has been important since ancient days. Ke'opuolani, Hawai'i's last pure-blooded sacred *ali'i*, was born here. She was a granddaughter of Maui's warrior king, Kekaulike, wife of Kamehameha the Conqueror, and the mother of two Hawaiian kings (Liholiho and Kauikeaouli—Kamehameha II and III, respectively), and of the tragic princess Nahi'ena'ena.

The historic heart of Wailuku lies near the old two-story Bailey House Museum, run by the Maui Historical Society. The house, built by missionaries in 1841, today offers a glimpse of missionary life, some pre-Western Hawaiian implements and artifacts, and a permanent exhibition of mid-nineteenth century Maui landscapes painted by the one-time owner of the house, Edward Bailey. Next door is a 1930s mansion built for the Wailuku Sugar Company's plantation manager, worth a stop for its evocative sense of Maui's plantation days. The landmark Ka'ahumanu Church, erected in 1876 on the site of an ancient *heiau*, is a short walk down Main Street from the museum.

At the corner of Main and Market, turn *makai,* toward the sea, on Market,

past the funky 'Iao Theater, which now houses the Maui Community Theater, to picturesque Vineyard Street. Several small restaurants cluster there, featuring Island, American, and Asian cuisine.

'Iao Valley State Park and the famous 'Iao Needle, Maui's most photographed natural landmark, are beyond Wailuku on Route 32. From the parking area beneath the Needle, several paved trails wind through tropical gardens to lovely 'Iao Stream. Beyond the Needle the valley ends in a great "amphitheater," with soaring cliffs, deep in the heart of the West Maui Mountains.

LOCATED ABOVE WAILUKU TOWN AND EASILY ACCESSIBLE BY AUTO, IS HISTORY-RICH 'IAO VALLEY. ON THIS SITE, BIG ISLAND CHIEF KAMEHAMEHA DEFEATED THE ARMY OF MAUI'S RULING CHIEF KALANIKUPULE.

The mouth of the valley, near the present Kepaniwai Park and Heritage Gardens, was the scene of a fierce battle between Maui's defending army under Chief Kalanikupule and the implacable forces of Kamehameha from the Big Island, who sealed his conquest of Maui here in 1790. Kepaniwai means "dammed waters." The 'Iao Stream is said to have been literally blocked with the bodies of fallen warriors. The defeated Maui chiefs, the dowager queen Kaola, and eleven-year-old princess Ke'opuolani fled into the valley and over the near-vertical cliffs to Olowalu near Lahaina, then by canoe to the island of Moloka'i.

Outside Wailuku on Highway 30 is the Maui Tropical Plantation at Waikapu, a popular visitor attraction. Its 120 acres showcase the variety of Hawai'i's crops, fruits, flowers, and exotics. Indoor exhibits explain the history, economics, and uses of Hawai'i's most famous agricultural exports.

Kanaha Beach Park near the Kahului airport is the area's busiest beach. When the trade winds are "up," this long and shady beach swarms with an international mob of windsurfers.

WAILUKU, THE COUNTY SEAT OF MAUI, IS OLDER THAN KAHULUI AND HAS THE ISLAND'S DEEP WATER PORT AND SHIPPING DOCKS.

ON THE WEST SIDE OF HIGH STREET, IN WAILUKU'S HISTORIC DISTRICT, IS MAUI'S EARLIEST EXISTING CHRISTIAN CHURCH. BUILT IN 1876, THE WHITE-PAINTED WOOD AND PLASTERED STONE KA'AHUMANU CHURCH ONCE HELD HAWAIIAN LANGUAGE SERVICES FOR A PRIMARILY HAWAIIAN CONGREGATION.

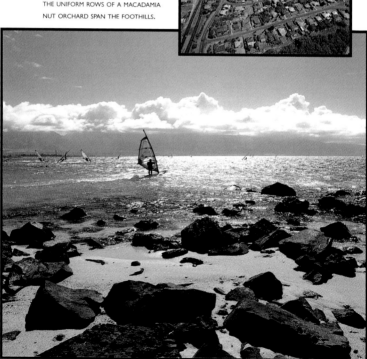

WAILUKU TOWN LOOKS AS IF IT IS SPILLING FROM THE MOUTH OF ʻIAO VALLEY IN THE WEST MAUI MOUNTAINS. LIGHT-GREEN PATCHES OF SUGAR CANE FLANK ITS LEFT SIDE, WHILE ON THE RIGHT THE UNIFORM ROWS OF A MACADAMIA NUT ORCHARD SPAN THE FOOTHILLS.

THE FAMED HOʻOKIPA BEACH PARK AND SURFING AREA NEAR THE SMALL COMMUNITY OF PAʻIA IS ALSO KNOWN AS HOʻOKIPA "LEFTS AND RIGHTS," DESCRIBING THE DIRECTION OF WAVES.

OLD WAILUKU RETAINS ITS UNIQUE 1890S FLAVOR WITH ITS STOREFRONT FACADES AND WOOD PLANK SIDEWALKS. LIFE IS STILL A BEAT SLOWER HERE, KEEPING TIME A BIT OUT OF STEP.

ON HIGHWAY 30, ON THE WAY TO KIHEI, WAILEA, LAHAINA, AND KAʻANAPALI, IS THE TROPICAL PLANTATION. VISITORS ARE INVITED INTO 120 ACRES OF LUSH FIELDS TO SEE A VARIETY OF HAWAIʻI'S FAMOUS CROPS, FLOWERS, AND EXOTICS CLOSE UP.

A HUGE VARIETY OF HIBISCUS GROW WILD, ALONG HIGHWAYS, IN CHURCH YARDS, AND FRONT YARDS, AND FROM SEA LEVEL UP TO 3,000 FEET HIGH IN THE MOUNTAINS.

"KING SUGAR" BEGAN ITS REIGN OVER ISLAND INDUSTRY IN THE 1860s, WHEN AMERICA'S CIVIL WAR BLOCKADES CUT OFF SOUTHERN SUGAR FROM WORLD MARKETS. PICTURED HERE IS THE PU'UNENE SUGAR MILL, STILL A FUNCTIONING PLANTATION.

Hamoa Beach

The white-sand crescent of Hamoa Beach is a unique sight along the lava-rough Hana Coast. The origin of the name "Hamoa" is not certain—it is believed to be a shortened version of Ha'amoa, which is an old name for Samoa. Access to the beach is on private property owned by the Hana Ranch, and since the 1930s Hamoa has been used soley by wealthy guests of the Hotel Hana Maui. Recently the general public was given access to the swimming area. Unprotected from the open sea, the surf off this 1,000-foot-long beach was a favorite surfing spot in ancient times and is listed as a "must surf" area when visiting Maui.

BEACHES

MAUI'S 120-MILE COASTLINE INCLUDES thirty-two miles of first-class beachfront. The longest stretches are on the western shores—eighteen miles of sand and calm water from Olowalu past Lahaina to Kapalua, and almost continuously from Ma'alaea through Kihei to Wailea near the southwestern corner of the island. In addition, coves with lovely beaches nestle among the cliffs and lava outcroppings at the island's extremities: north of Kapalua, at Hana, and south of Wailea. The north-shore beaches are smaller and less inviting for visitors because of pounding surf and stiff winds, which create unending erosion problems. Twenty-four state and county beach parks dot Maui's shoreline. Few have lifeguards, but most have restrooms, freshwater showers, and parking.

Maui has at least one beach to satisfy every taste. Surfers gravitate to Ho'okipa, Ma'alaea, Honolua, and Lahaina. Bodysurfers head for Slaughterhouse, Makena, Hamoa, and Baldwin Beach. Windsurfers call Maui mecca, and Ho'okipa, Ma'alaea, and Kanaha are its top shrines. Sunbathers have their secret coves or they simply step out of their hotels, which are situated on a vast majority of Maui's most placid swimming and sunning beaches. When the sea is calm, snorkelers have an unmatched selection of sand-and-rocky-point configurations, particularly at Wailea and Makena in South Maui, Pu'u Keka'a at Ka'anapali, and at Kapalua, Honolua, and Fleming beaches near Kapalua.

A "menu" of Maui's best-known, best-loved and best-kept-secret beaches follows. By all means, spend a complete day at one of them, preferably facing west to the sunset. Take plenty of food and water, a beach umbrella, heavy-duty sun screen, swim fins and snorkel, a book or two, a long-sleeve shirt, and long pants. (Right after sunset you'll feel chilly.)

Note: All beaches in Hawai'i are public up to the vegetation line above the high-water mark. Rights-of-way to the beach from public roads are marked (some better than others), even in exclusive beachfront residential areas and resorts.

Words of Caution

Depending on surf conditions, any Hawaiian beach can be dangerous. Placid water sometimes hides dangerous currents. Exciting shore waves, full of bobbing heads, pack a wallop that can injure—even kill—unsuspecting or inexperienced swimmers.

Coral, abundant in shallow water around Maui, is a common source of abrasions and lacerations. Swimmers, surfers, and divers sometimes encounter drifting Portuguese man-of-war, whose long trailers cause painful stings and occasionally serious allergy problems. If you see the translucent blue bubbles of the Portuguese man-of-war washed up on the beach, avoid stepping on them. Chances are they're in the water, too.

Makena Beach aka Big Beach aka Oneloa Beach

WHICHEVER NAME IT GOES BY, THIS ISOLATED, END-OF-THE-ROAD SPOT IS MAUI'S FAVORITE. THE WATER IS CLEAR, THE VIEWS ARE WIDE-OPEN. THERE IS NO SIGN OF CIVILIZATION ANYWHERE, AND THE "SHORE-BREAK" WAVES USUALLY RANGE BETWEEN FRISKY AND CHALLENGING. MAKENA BEACH GAINED FAME IN THE LATE 1960S AS A BACK-TO-NATURE COLONY. SANITATION AND OTHER PROBLEMS FINALLY FORCED POLICE AND HEALTH OFFICIALS TO CLOSE IT DOWN. THE ONLY REMINDER OF THOSE DAYS IS LITTLE BEACH, A SANDY COVE REACHED BY A SHORT TRAIL FROM THE END OF BIG BEACH, WHERE FREE SPIRITS CONTINUE TO SUNBATHE IN THE BUFF. SNORKELING OFF THE ROCKY POINTS AT MAKENA AND LITTLE BEACH IS FANTASTIC. ALMOST ANY TIME BETWEEN NOVEMBER AND MARCH, A FEW FEET BENEATH THE SURFACE MIGHT BE HEARD THE FAINT, HIGH-PITCHED CLICKS, MOANS, AND WHISTLES OF THE HUMPBACK WHALES, WHOSE "SONGS" TRAVEL FOR MILES UNDERWATER.

Maui's popular beaches—particularly those protected from the wind by mountains and from the surf by offshore reefs—are generally safe. But along less-developed coasts, where cliffs and small coves predominate, always be very cautious. Strong shore currents can surprise even good swimmers. When no one else is around, stay out of the water.

Swim fins ("flippers") give swimmers one-third more power and should help you really enjoy Hawai'i's vibrant waters. Swimmers' goggles are a less-bulky alternative to the standard mask-and-snorkel and allow you more swimming freedom while inspecting Cousteau land. Both are available at surf and dive shops and some drug stores and supermarkets.

Lastly, please treat Maui's beaches as the very special places they are. Make sure everything you brought to the beach goes back with you when you leave. *Mahalo.*

Ho'okipa Beach Park

RIGHT ALONGSIDE THE HANA HIGHWAY BEYOND PA'IA,
HO'OKIPA IS THE BEST-KNOWN SURFING AND
WINDSURFING BEACH ON MAUI. BIG WINTER SURF ROLLS
INTO THE SHALLOW BAY AND BREAKS ACROSS THE
BEACHFRONT, NOT A HUNDRED YARDS OFFSHORE. BIG-
WAVE WINDSURFING WAS VIRTUALLY INVENTED HERE.
WINDSURFERS AND BOARD SURFERS NOW DIVIDE THE
WAVES (WINDSURFERS TO THE LEFT; BOARD SURFERS TO
THE RIGHT). SPECTATORS GET A DOUBLE THRILL
WATCHING SURFERS AND THEIR WIND-BORNE
COUNTERPARTS ON THE SAME WAVES.

Kaihalulu Beach

In calm sea conditions, this hidden gem of a beach on the far right side of Ka'uiki Hill in Hana has some of the best, most intimate snorkeling in the state. It's like swimming in an aquarium. Carved from the volcanic cinder cone that created Ka'uiki Hill, Kaihalulu cove is often called Red Sand Beach. The blue water lapping against the reddish sand is stunningly beautiful. Although the small beach is protected from direct sea action by a jagged lava barrier, swimmers should still exercise caution.

Ka'anapali Beach

MAUI'S RESORT BEACH PAR EXCELLENCE, KA'ANAPALI IS A BROAD, THREE-MILE EXPANSE OF GOLDEN SAND, INVITING WATER, AND IS TERRIFIC FOR PEOPLE WATCHING. THERE'S LITTLE SOLITUDE HERE. KA'ANAPALI IS FOR SOCIAL BEACH-GOING, SEEING, AND BEING SEEN. THE BUSIEST PART FRONTS THE LIVELY RESTAURANTS AT WHALER'S VILLAGE BETWEEN KA'ANAPALI BEACH HOTEL AND THE WESTIN MAUI. DURING THE DAY, A SAND VOLLEYBALL COURT DRAWS THE DEEPLY-TANNED MUSCLE CROWD AND THE THICKEST CONCENTRATION OF SINGLES. AS THE SUN SINKS IN A BLAZE OF COLOR BEHIND A DISTANT ISLAND, AND MUSIC DRIFTS OUT TO THE BEACH, COUPLES PLAY OUT THEIR DREAMS OF A COCKTAIL AND A BAREFOOT WALK IN THE SAND.

HOBIE-CAT SAILING IS ONE OF THE MANY ACTIVITIES OFFERED AT THE KAʻANAPALI RESORT COMPLEX. EXPERIENCED INSTRUCTORS TEACH NOVICE SAILORS IN THE PLACID WATERS OF THE PAILOLO CHANNEL BETWEEN THE ISLANDS OF MAUI AND MOLOKAʻI.

THE CONSTANT GUSTING OF THE TRADEWINDS AND THE FORCE OF THE OPEN OCEAN WAVES COMBINE TO MAKE MAUI WINDSURFING THE BEST IN THE WORLD.

ADVENTURES

IF YOUR VACATION REQUIRES more than a memorable tan, Maui offers snorkeling off your hotel beach, deep-sea fishing, windsurfing, sailing, kayaking, hiking, bicycling down Haleakalā, horseback riding, scuba diving on Molokini, or cruising to Lana'i.

Maui's calm leeward ocean, enclosed by four islands, provides the most scenic, hospitable, and comfortable sailing water in the state. From November to April these same waters are the winter home of the North Pacific's humpback whales. A wide variety of charter boats are available for whale-watching, sailing, diving, fishing, and sightseeing. Other craft, large and small, offer sunset dinner cruises. Most commercial boating operations are based at Lahaina and Ma'alaea harbors, close to West Maui resorts.

High-energy wind and sea conditions, plus year-round warm weather, make Maui a natural for the athletically inclined. The island has become one of the world's great water-sports capitals, with international surfing contests, long-distance swimming meets, offshore fishing tournaments, inter-island canoe and kayak races, windsurfing competitions, and inter-island and trans-Pacific yacht races. On shore, brawny "triathletes," daring hang-glider pilots, and mud-stained hikers carry the "just do it" ethos to new extremes. International golf and tennis tournaments proliferate, and the Maui invitational basketball

THE MAN HOLDING THIS PUFFER FISH RELEASED IT SOON AFTER THIS PHOTO WAS TAKEN.

POWERFUL OCEAN CURRENTS AND THE BLUSTERING OF
TRADE WINDS HAVE MADE THE ONCE UNKNOWN HO'OKIPA
BEACH A MECCA FOR WINDSURFERS

tournament draws athletes from colleges across the United States.

On Maui, there is energy everywhere—in the big mid-Pacific water, in the stiff trade winds, and on this young volcanic island itself. Everything converges with spectacular power and astonishing gentleness. You can *feel* the vibrant energy as soon as you arrive.

THE GENTLE HUMPBACK WHALES, ONCE HUNTED OFF THE COAST OF LAHAINA, NOW MIGRATE FROM THE NORTH PACIFIC TO THE WARM WATERS OF HAWAI'I TO CALVE THEIR YOUNG. SMALL BOATS CONDUCT WHALE-WATCHING TOURS FROM LAHAINA, MA'ALAEA, AND KIHEI TO DEVELOP AWARENESS AND EDUCATE VISITORS ABOUT THE LIFE AND BEHAVIOR OF THESE SEAGOING MAMMALS. *PHOTO BY MIKE NOLAN*

✳   ✳   ✳

Note: *Kapu* (taboo, beware, avoid). The recent proliferation of "thrill craft"—jetskis, parasail rides, speedboats, dune buggies, and other devices that have no transportation purpose except the mechanical ride itself—has generated alarm and resentment in Hawai'i. As a visitor, you should be aware of how intrusive the noise, air pollution, danger, and general blight from these activities are to other users of Hawai'i's waters, forests, and mountains.

Their threat to endangered sea and plant life makes them the subject of very serious concern among not only local environmentalists, but others who wish to defend Hawai'i's natural spirit and integrity. This attitude is called *aloha 'aina*, love for the land. We hope you will respect and share it.

Whale-Watching

Whale-watching is Maui's premier seasonal attraction. The island-protected leeward waters are a natural amphitheater for the migratory North Pacific humpback whales that leave coastal Alaska in the fall and arrive in November.

During their stay until April to calve and mate, the whales eat little (living off their blubber for six months). But they do sing. To hear them is one of Maui's unique experiences. Simply swim into some open, calm water at least 10 feet deep anywhere along Maui's south-western shores during the winter. Take a deep breath and sink a foot or two beneath the surface, holding perfectly still. If any whales are around, you'll hear high-pitched whistles, low moans and clicking sounds—forty-ton intelligent mammals communicating with each other, a mile to maybe five miles away.

Whales usually can be spotted by the plumes of mist or "spouts" they shoot into the air as they exhale. Occasionally a humpback will repeatedly jump almost clear of the water. This "breaching" is tremendously exciting to watch. If you go on a whale-watching charter or simply watch from shore, be sure to take binoculars and a good telephoto lens for your camera.

Federal and State regulations protect the endangered humpbacks from harassment. All boats, except bona fide research vessels, must maintain a minimum distance of 100 yards.

During whale season, Lahaina and Ma'alaea harbors are filled with sailboats, catamarans, fishing craft, and big excursion boats offering chances to view the whales in well-provisioned comfort. Sightings cannot be guaranteed, but are frequent enough to keep the mini-industry flourishing. Excursions usually last about four hours and may include a light breakfast, lunch, or sunset dinner. There are several ocean sports operations that offer excursions out of Ma'alaea and Lahaina. A number of sleek 36-foot catamarans and a few sailing yachts take groups out over the "whale roads." Prices vary, depending on the length of the sail and food service. Private charters are available by advance reservation.

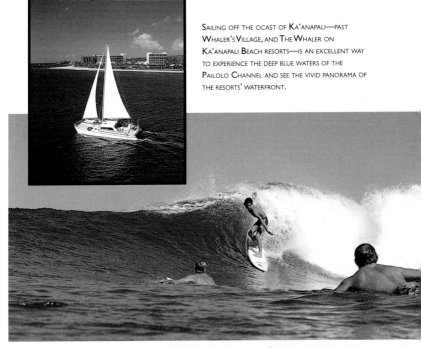

SAILING OFF THE OCAST OF KA'ANAPALI—PAST WHALER'S VILLAGE, AND THE WHALER ON KA'ANAPALI BEACH RESORTS—IS AN EXCELLENT WAY TO EXPERIENCE THE DEEP BLUE WATERS OF THE PAILOLO CHANNEL AND SEE THE VIVID PANORAMA OF THE RESORTS' WATERFRONT.

HONOLUA BAY USED TO BE A SECRET SPOT FOR LOCALS ONLY. THE TUBULAR "RIGHTS" OF THE STRONG NORTH SWELLS IN WINTER MAKE THIS ONE OF THE BEST HIGH-PERFORMANCE BREAKS ON THE ISLAND.

On Foot

The best hiking and walking on Maui are either at the summit or on the broad, lower slopes of Haleakalā. Two mildly demanding options are worth special notice. One is through Polipoli State Park's highland forests. The other is into Haleakalā's surreal, lunar-like summit crater. Several other short hikes are listed in the "Tours" section of this volume. Note particularly one along the Hana coast at Waikamoi State Park and another at the waterfalls to 'Ohe'o Gulch in Kipahulu.

THE WAI'ANAPANAPA TRAIL, ALONG THE HANA COAST, IS BLANKETED WITH *HALA* LEAVES. FERNS, *TI* PLANTS, AND A VARIETY OF TREES SHADE THE TRANQUIL SETTING AS CRASHING WAVES BOOM ONTO NEARBY WAI'ANAPANAPA BEACH.

✻　　　✻　　　✻

Polipoli State Park, a remote forest sanctuary high above the gardens of Kula at the 6,200-foot level on Haleakalā, is one of Maui's least-visited parks. The latter half of the ten-mile road into the park is unpaved and often severely rutted. Four-wheel-drive vehicles are recommended, although in good weather regular cars usually can make it.

Polipoli has a unique mixture of native and introduced plant species. Redwoods planted at the turn of the century, cypress groves, stands of eucalyptus, cryptomeria pines, and *Acacia koa* predominate. Fog and clouds regularly cloak the high trees and muffle the cries of pheasant and grouse. In addition to game birds, the feral pigs and wild goats make this area popular with hunters. This is one place where Hawai'i doesn't look anything like what you expected.

The entrance to the park is marked. The trails are well signed, including mileage information for day hikes (the Redwood Trail is recommended). Seasonal pig and bird hunting requires a license. An overnight cabin with a camp stove and bunks for ten is available. To reserve space call the State Parks office in Wailuku. Polipoli State Park is reached via Route 377, past the Kula Botanical Garden to a left turn on Waipoli Road.

Haleakalā. Thirty-six miles of hiking trails crisscross Haleakalā National Park, but most of them are for overnighters. Day-trippers are pretty well restricted to leaving from and returning to either of two places. Sliding Sands Trail starts at the visitor center at the summit, the Halemau'u Trail from the parking lot at the 8,000-foot level on the road to the summit. For information on weather and mileage, check in at park headquarters or at the summit visitor center.

The Sliding Sands Trail descends to the crater floor's multi-hued cinder cones. Distances are deceiving in this otherworldly landscape. What looks like a quick jaunt is often an hours-long journey. To reach the floor and return to the rim requires a full day, so turn back *before* your energy runs out. The uphill, high-altitude return climb on this "sliding" trail can be exhausting. Be sure to pack water for this trip.

The Halemau'u trail to Holua Cabin is an eight-mile, six-hour roundtrip. The first mile descends from

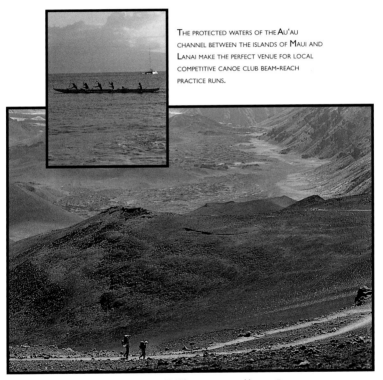

THE PROTECTED WATERS OF THE AUʻAU CHANNEL BETWEEN THE ISLANDS OF MAUI AND LANAI MAKE THE PERFECT VENUE FOR LOCAL COMPETITIVE CANOE CLUB BEAM-REACH PRACTICE RUNS.

EACH YEAR THOUSANDS OF VISITORS DRIVE TO THE 10,023-FOOT SUMMIT OF HALEAKALĀ IN THE PREDAWN HOURS TO WITNESS THE SUNRISE. OTHER MORE ADVENTUROUS SOULS REMAIN TO HIKE THE AUSTERE ENVIRONS. THE CRATER, AN EROSION OF VOLCANIC MATERIAL, MEASURES 21 MILES IN CIRCUMFERENCE, 3,000 FEET DEEP, AND 19 SQUARE MILES IN DIAMETER.

the parking lot through alpine scrubland to the rim, then the trail descends in a series of dramatic switchbacks and across a meadow to the cabin. The views of Haleakalā's northern flanks, the lava rivers of cloud-wrapped Ko'olau Gap, and the moist cliffs of Leleiwi are the prime rewards of this popular hike.

DESCENDING THE 10,000-FOOT HALEAKALĀ SUMMIT TO SEA LEVEL WITHOUT PEDALING MAY NOT BE THE PERFECT ACTIVITY FOR EVERYONE, BUT THIS ULTIMATE BIKE RIDE IS CERTAINLY A RUSH YOU'LL NEVER FORGET.

❊   ❊   ❊

Overnight hikes into the corners of Haleakalā's vast summit crater require careful planning, adequate camping gear, rainwear, food, and water. The Kapalaoa, Paliku, and Holua overnight cabins and campsites at Paliku and Holua are the focuses of overnight trips. The cabins should be reserved three months in advance by writing the Superintendent, Haleakalā National Park. Campers must register at park headquarters before setting out.

Bicycling Down Haleakalā
Bob Kiger, a retired Hollywood ad man, on his birthday in 1983 took his bike to the 10,000-foot summit of Haleakalā so he could coast down 38 twisting miles to the seashore town of Pa'ia. Inspired by his experience, he bought a few mountain bikes, developed special "megabrakes," and opened a business. Today several companies offer the spectacular trip in small escorted

groups on special mountain bikes with very fancy brakes, helmets, rain gear, hearty breakfasts, picnic lunches, guides, escort vans, hotel pick-up service, and lots of insurance. The six-hour descent is carefree, the pace is reasonable, and the scenery dizzyingly beautiful. The commercial operators require strict adherence to a 20-mph speed limit, permit no passing once in line, and require frequent stops to let cars pass. Children must be big enough to straddle a 26-inch cruiser bike; those under 16 require a parental release.

Most of the bike-ride opera-tions offer trips at sunrise, midday, and sunset, and bad-weather insurance. The cost may seem as steep as the mountain, but it's a bargain for such a once-in-a-lifetime thrill.

Snorkeling
Of all Hawai'i's islands, Maui is the best for novice snorkelers. The coves north of Ka'anapali and south of Kihei, characterized by sand bottoms between low lava "arms" or points, are perfect for easy snorkeling. Getting into the water via the beach and swimming to the points is easy. The underwater rocks, reefs, and coral are ideal for watching butterflyfish,

tangs, Moorish idols, wrasse, surgeonfish, *manini,* the famous *humuhumu-nukunukuapua'a* (Hawai'i's state fish), ulua, parrotfish, green sea turtles, moray eels, spiny lobsters, sea shrimp, *wana* (sea urchins—don't touch!), and colorful coral colonies.

The very best beaches for snorkeling are at Makena and Wailea, at Kamaole Beach Parks II and III in Kihei, Olowalu, and Pu'u Keka'a (Black Rock) at Ka'anapali Beach. Kapalua, Slaughterhouse Beach, and Honolua, at the northern end of the West Maui coastline, are excellent during placid summer weather. In winter, these exposed areas are frequently rough, dangerous, and no fun for a novice.

The most popular offshore snorkeling is at Molokini Islet, a small volcanic crescent about three miles off the Makena shore. Every morning a fleet of commercial tour boats heads for the island's little bay for a few hours of snorkeling and an early lunch. Thousands of reef fish tamed by regular feedings literally eat bread out of your hand—environmentally questionable, perhaps, but great for photography. Most operators rent underwater cameras.

As Molokini's popularity and crowds have increased, some commercial snorkeling tours have opted for Hulopo'e Bay Marine Preserve and other secluded coves on the island of Lana'i. A number of ocean activities businesses, operating out of Lahaina and Kihei offer a range of daily group excursions to Molokini and Lana'i from Ma'alaea Harbor. You'll receive snorkeling equipment, breakfast, lunch, and some lively demonstrations of sea life.

THE MORNING SUN RISING ABOVE THE CREST OF HALEAKALĀ BLANCHES THE EMPTY BEACH FRONTING THE COMMUNITY OF KIHEI.

This sperm whale skeleton on display at Whaler's Village in Ka'anapali was erected to commemorate the area's history and to remind all who live and visit here of our connection to the mammals of the sea.

An 'ipu, Hawaiian percussion instrument used to accompany kahiko (ancient) hula and chant, is made from a hollowed and polished bottle gourd. The chanter thumps different parts of the rounded bottom and neck to vary the pitch of the drumming.

Planet Hollywood, the movie stars' answer to Hard Rock Cafe, opened its Lahaina shop in 1995 in an old Front Street building.

MAUI CIVILIZATION

THERE ARE TWO WAYS to spend your time and money on Maui: staying close to the resorts or mingling with the local residents. The Kapalua, Ka'anapali, and Wailea master-planned resorts include excellent shops and galleries, posh restaurants, carefully crafted pools, and romantic bars. But forty minutes beyond the resort gates, there are smaller and less expensive restaurants, shops and watering places that offer some down-to-earth alternatives.

In Wailuku's spirited bars and Upcountry Maui's cozy lodges, "locals" and visitors mix freely. From Kahului's general-purpose shopping to Makawao's casually chic dining and Pa'ia's artsy-craftsy browsing, you'll find there is much more to Maui than pricey lobster tails and logo-covered beach towels.

Shopping

At the high end are the **Kapalua Shops** at Kapalua, **Whalers' Village** at Ka'anapali and **Wailea Shopping Village** at Wailea—collections of resort shops for top-drawer browsing and buying. Although more plebian, **Lahaina** can also be a fabulous place for shopping. Countless **Front Street** vendors sell silly t-shirts, beachwear, scrimshaw jewelry, knickknacks, bric-a-brac, whirligig hats, and other cleverly useless items. For inexpensive gifts to take home for a few laughs, these shops can't be beat. And Front Street is like a carnival for people-watching—there's even a tattoo shop. Lahaina's most interesting mini-malls include **505 Front Street**, the **Wharf**, **844 Front Street**, and the **Cannery**.

MAUI BOASTS SOME OF THE FINEST RESTAURANTS IN THE WORLD, OFFERING EVERY TYPE OF CUISINE FROM NOUVELLE TO ORIENTAL, WESTERN TO ITALIAN.

On the opposite side of the island, **Kahului** has the best general shopping. Along Ka'ahumanu Avenue and geared to the local market is the **Ka'ahumanu Shopping Center** (the biggest, with Sears and Liberty House, Hawai'i's leading department store), **Maui Mall,** and **Kahului Shopping Center**. Prices here are lower than in the resort areas, so Kahului is your best bet for standard beachgear, books, food for your condo, and maybe clothes.

ALOHA CANTINA, ONE OF LAHAINA'S MORE INTERESTING EATERIES, OFFERS A MEXICAN MENU OF TACOS AND BURRITOS, TOSTADAS AND MARGARITAS.

✳   ✳   ✳

Specialty shops are worth seeking out, and they are all over the island. Indeed, Maui is a mecca for artists and craftsmen, and you will find in their shops everything from hand-painted silks to woven baskets, Hawaiian quilts, books, musical instruments, recorded music, handmade clothes to surfing equipment and beachwear, and astonishing original collectibles made from fibers, woods, clays, and glass. In Makawao you'll even find a Western general store-style outfitter for the area's real cowboys.

Art Galleries

Maui's thriving art scene is a study in contrasts. Along Lahaina's Front Street, Red Skelton's clown paintings, "Dali" prints, and hundreds of dolphin interpretations share window space with sublime landscapes and sensuous flower studies. By all the evidence, Maui's art market is booming, but sometimes it's hard to figure out how much is actually art and how much is just market.

The theme of much of Maui's commercial art is the underwater environment featuring whales, dolphins, reef fish, and lots of blue paint. The international success of **Robert Wyland**, whose huge, inspiring whale murals can be seen around the world, as well as the immense popularity of **Robert Lyn Nelson's** work, has spawned a school of marine art whose headquarters is Maui, whale-watching capital of the world. Wyland/Nelson imitators are plentiful and it's fascinating to tour the galleries, most of them along Front Street, just to see their work.

Among Maui's better artists are **Curtis Wilson Cost, Pamela Andelin, George Allan, Eddie Flotte, Margaret Bedell,** and **Ian Tremewen.** You can find these and other talented painters at galleries all over the island.

BARTENDERS WILL SHAKE, BLEND, OR STIR ANY CONCOCTION YOUR IMAGINATION CAN CREATE.

HALI'IMAILI GENERAL STORE AND CAFE IN UPCOUNTRY MAUI NEAR THE TOWN OF MAKAWAO HAS AN INVENTIVE MENU AND ART-COVERED WALLS.

WEST MAUI'S ARTIST COMMUNITY HAS FLOURISHED AND THE NUMBER OF GALLERIES IN THE AREA HAS DOUBLED.

Local Events

For data on local music and cultural events, fairs, community *lu'au*, and special celebrations, see the daily *Maui News* "Datebook" and "Calendar of Events" columns. Look for a community fundraising *lu'au* if you want the real flavor and spirit of Hawaiian feasting.

✳   ✳   ✳   ✳

SHADOWS OF TWILIGHT COOL THE BEACH AT WAILEA AS THE SUN DESCENDS BEHIND THE WEST MAUI MOUNTAINS. WITH THE COMING OF NIGHT, THE SOUNDS OF THE LAPPING SHOREBREAK AND GENTLY RUFFLING PALM FRONDS BECKON THOSE WITH ROMANTIC HEARTS TO WALK ALONG THE TALK-SOFT SANDS IN THE STARLIGHT.